D1537483

25 Advent Legends from around the world with matching ornaments

By Judith Vicary Swisher

Illustrations by Nancy Middlebrook Baay

For our children and grandchildren

Published 2008
Second Printing
ISBN #978-0-615-21795-6

Copyright 2008
Judith Vicary Swisher
Nancy Middlebrook Baay

Published by Rogers Press
Printed by Everbest Printing Company in China through Four Colour Imports, Louisville, KY

Introduction

Many years ago when a young Danish girl lived with us, we asked about her country's holiday customs – Saint Lucia celebration on December 13th. And then I began collecting more Christmas legends from around the world to share with my children each night of Advent. We made ornaments to match each story and hung them on a special tree as we read the legends. The tradition continued, even as everyone became 'too old' for such customs. Then came the grandchildren and my son asked why I hadn't yet published the stories. He wanted his children to share the tradition, and so Celebrate Advent became a book, one to share with other families. I hope you too can start a family tradition for your Christmas season, enjoying the hope and message from so many lands.

Angels

The angel Gabriel was sent by God to Nazareth, a city in Galilee, to a young woman named Mary who was living there. The angel came to her and said, "Hail, O favored one, the Lord is with you. Do not be afraid for you have found favor with God. And behold you will bear a son, and you shall call his name Jesus. He will be great and will be called the Son of the Most High." Mary said "Let it be to me according to your word."

After Mary and Joseph went to Bethlehem to be enrolled, the time came for the baby's birth. Suddenly an angel of the Lord appeared to the shepherds, and the glory of the Lord shone around them. And the angel said to them "This day a Saviour is born to you, and you will find him wrapped in swaddling clothes in a manger." And in the heavens there was a multitude of angels praising God, saying "Glory to God in the highest, and on earth peace among men."

Birds

Many years ago a raven was flying high in the sky one night, when suddenly the sky was filled with the glory of angels all around. They told the raven the joyous news of Christ's birth in Bethlehem. He flew off at once to tell all the other birds of this glorious gift to the world. Immediately the birds began to celebrate and plan how to welcome the babe. The little wren knew she could weave a small blanket made of feathers, green leaves, and moss to keep the baby comfortable. For this she is known today as the "bird of God" in many lands.

Meanwhile the nightingale, with his glorious voice, sang a lovely lullaby. In thanks God blessed him, saying that his song would be forever the sweetest in the world, and the only one heard the whole night through. Today, in remembrance of these gifts, birds in many places like Scandinavia, Hungary, and Poland are given a special treat at Christmastime. There, bird trees hold sheaves of grain, corn or wheat, put out in thanks for their care for the Christ Child.

Babushka

A legend is told in Russia, and in Poland and Italy too, of a grandmotherly old woman who was snug in her room one cold winter night many years ago. Suddenly there was a knock at her door, and three men in glorious robes came in, telling Babushka that in Bethlehem a special baby had been born in a lowly stable. "Please come with us to see this child, who came to the world to be the Prince of Peace. Bring a basket of things to help the little one," they said. But the woman was warm and comfortable in her cottage and refused to go out in the cold with the three wise men.

She did promise though to come the next morning, and then climbed into her warm bed while they went on to find the Christ Child.

The next morning Babushka packed a basket full of gifts for the little one, with a warm cover for his mother, and went to find the baby in the stable. But when she got there it was already empty, and the holy family was gone. And since that day she has traveled the world, peering in each child's face trying to find the Christ Child. At Christmastime she leaves gifts for each one, always hoping that one will be that child, born in a manger that she didn't find so long ago.

Shepherds

In the region near where Mary and Joseph rested in the stable, shepherds were out in the fields at night, watching over their flocks. These poor and humble men had to care for their animals in cold and difficult conditions. Then suddenly an angel of the Lord appeared to them, saying, "Be not afraid, for to you is born this day a Savior who is Christ the Lord. This shall be a sign for you. The babe is wrapped in swaddling clothes lying in a manger."

In awe and hope, the shepherds decided to go to Bethlehem to see what the Lord had made known to them. They hurried through the night with their flocks, and found the babe in the manger, just as the angels had told them. After worshiping the child they returned home, glorifying and praising God for all they had heard and seen, as it had been told to them.

Stork

When the baby Christ was born on Christmas Day many years ago, animals and birds gathered around in wonder. The wild creatures flocked to the manger where the Christ Child lay. And of all the birds there, one stood especially tall. It was the long-legged stork, with feathers so white and a crest on her head held high. But this lovely creature felt very sad when she saw the poor, cold place where the child slept.

Then she had an idea and knew what she could do to make a cozy bed like the one where her own children had slept. She carefully plucked the down feathers from her chest, pulling out the plumes so the child wouldn't sleep in such a hard place. The stork made the manger soft and warm with her feathers, a bed fit for a king. And ever since the stork has been blessed for the gift of her body's feathers to the baby. Today she is now known as the patron of babies everywhere.

Cat

On that wondrous night when Jesus was born, all the wild creatures, beasts and birds alike, left their lairs and nests and traveled in silent wonder to pay homage to the babe. Cat came too, a shy and wild creature. It lay near by, no closer than the hearth, while the other animals knelt closer in peaceful reverence. Cat was overcome by the glory and could only gaze at the child, quietly purring a soft sound.

In the morning all the other animals silently left, returning to their own habitats, leaving Cat near the manger and hearth. Seeing this, Mary spoke to the wild creature, blessing him for staying with them. She said, "Now leave the wilderness behind, and from now on, be where people are, bringing warmth to many a family. Tho' you will never be a servant, yet you are forever bound to home and humankind." Today, as Cat stands and stretches, he remembers those wild days but then settles back content by the human hearth, again purring a song of joy.

Candles

In medieval times there was a legend that told the story of the Christ Child wandering throughout the world on Christmas Eve. He was said to look for places where he would be welcomed and sheltered. People then lit candles and put them in their windows to show him the way. But how would he appear? Perhaps as a beggar, an old man, or a homeless child? The message tells us no one should be turned away from the light of Christ when there is always room for him in our hearts.

Today people put candles in their windows to say "welcome" to any weary traveler far from home at Christmastime. Who knows, perhaps the Christ Child will come their way  one day. Another old legend, from Germany, says that Mary and a host of angels pass over the countryside on Christmas Eve, blessing those homes where they see the candles. We also light candles with our Advent wreaths, representing the four weeks of Advent and Christmas Day. These lightings symbolize the expectation and hope of the season of Christ's birth.

Drummer Boy

When the Christ Child was born so many years ago, people who heard of his birth brought gifts to him in the stable. Like those gifts of the wise men, there were presents of great beauty, splendor, and value. One small boy also came to worship Jesus, but he had no gift to give, being very poor. He felt very sad and wondered what he could do? Since he was only a small child he had no idea what the Christ Child would like.

Then he thought, "What makes me happy? Why, music of course! So perhaps I can play my drum for him, and make him happy." And then he played. Pa-rum-pum-pum, pa-rum-pum-pum went his little drum. He played with all his heart and with all the love he felt for the small child. And, as the boy played, the baby Jesus smiled and laughed, and the little Drummer Boy then knew his gift from the heart was the best gift of all that one could give.

Robin

A small brown bird once flew into the stable to see where the Christ Child lay. As Jesus and his parents lay sleeping, the warm fire there started to fade away and the manger became colder and colder. The little robin wondered what she could do to warm the baby. How could she help build up the fire? Then she had an idea. She flew down from the rafters and began to fan the embers with her wings. Throughout the night she was going to keep the fire going, so that the baby Jesus would be warm.

But the robin soon realized the wind was blowing sparks from the fire nearer and nearer the sleeping child. "I know what I can do now," she thought. "I can catch the hot sparks on my breast, so the baby doesn't get burned." So all night long she spread her wings and caught the sparks on her own brown breast, which was red by dawn. In the morning, the child's mother saw what the robin had done and thanked her gratefully, saying, "From this day on your red breast will tell the world of your kindness, your gift to this Child of Bethlehem."

Holly

Holly bushes once bore only a small white bloom each year beside their thorny leaves. One such bush grew by the stable door where the baby Jesus lay years ago in that lowly manger. When the Christ Child was born, villagers gathered round his bedside, bringing gifts as best they could afford. But one very poor lad who came to see the child had nothing to give. All he could think to do was to take a prickly branch of the nearby holly tree and weave it into a wreath as his lowly gift.

The boy took his gift to the child but as the baby reached out to touch it, a spiny leaf pricked his finger, leaving a drop of blood on the bloom. The boy was so ashamed and began to cry, and as his tears fell they turned into scarlet berries. Mary said, "You have both shown care for my Son, so all the holly's thorny leaves are forgiven and your berries shall always turn red, rejoicing in the birth of Christ." Today the holly bush is an important part of our Christmas joy in remembrance of this blessing.

Animals in the Stable

As the story is told, the Christ Child was born in a humble stable in Bethlehem, where the family went to be registered by the government. But they could not find any place with room for them. Finally, an innkeeper allowed them to stay in his stable. When the Christ Child was born there, the little family was not alone. Joseph, Mary, and Jesus were surrounded by friendly beasts for company. These lowly creatures welcomed the young child and his parents with all their hearts.

One young donkey had proudly carried Mary to Bethlehem as they traveled that long distance. The sheep with the curly horn gave him wool for his warm blanket, while the cattle let the child lie in the manger with their hay for his pillow. The cow even breathed on the baby to help keep him warm. Now legend tells us that at midnight on Christmas Eve all the animals in the stable kneel in adoration of the Christ Child. And for one brief time they are given the gift of speech as thanks for their kindness. Perhaps they tell again of the gifts from their hearts that they gave that first Christmas night.

Stocking

The first Saint Nicholas was a bishop in Asia Minor in the fourth century, in an area that is part of Turkey today. A kind nobleman lived there too, with his three daughters. After his wife died, the family fell into poverty. The man was afraid he might have to sell his daughters into slavery, because he didn't have the money to provide them with a dowry so that they could marry. The bishop, who became Saint Nicholas, heard about their bad fortune and wished to aid them. But he wanted to do it secretly so that no one would know who had helped the young girls.

One evening after the daughters had washed their clothes, hung them to dry by the fireplace, and gone to bed, the bishop saw their stockings through a window. He had an idea then of how he could give them all a gift for a dowry. Three times he threw gifts of small bags of gold down the poor man's chimney, and each time one bag of gold landed, one in each daughter's stocking. So even today children hang up their stockings on Christmas Eve, hoping that they will be full of gifts by morning. In some countries like France and Germany, a wooden shoe is used instead.

Saint Lucia

Hundreds of years ago, a wealthy young girl lived in Sicily. The night before she was to be married, Lucia announced that she had become a Christian and would give all her money away to help the poor people in her village buy food. For this she was accused of being a witch and was killed.

Another legend about Saint Lucia says that she also helped poor Christians in hiding because of their faith

by bringing them food and drink. In order to keep her hands free to carry as much as possible, she wore a wreath on her head to which she had attached candles to see by in the dark hiding places. To honor these sacrifices, the oldest daughter in a Scandinavian family today dresses in a white robe on December 13, Santa Lucia Day. Wearing a wreath of greens and lights on her head, she brings coffee and holiday buns to her family in the early morning.

Christmas Rose

When the shepherds guarding their flocks in the hills heard that the Christ Child was born in a stable in Bethlehem, they hurried there to see him. With them came a little shepherdess, a young girl who also had come to the manger to worship the child. When they arrived, the girl saw that others were there with their rich gifts, and she began to cry because she had no gift for the baby.

As her tears fell to the ground, a beautiful white flower sprang up from each tear. The little shepherdess

was surprised at first. But then she gathered up the flowers into a small bouquet and shyly gave them to the mother and child. Mary smiled at the girl, thanking her for her caring gift, and the baby reached out, touching the roses. Where he touched them, a beautiful pink color appeared on the petals. These flowers are now forever known as the Christmas Rose, in honor of the shepherdess's loving gift.

Spider Web

Many years after Christ was born, people brought small pine trees into their homes to decorate for the Christmas holidays. One year a poor family had no money to spare and could not afford the beautiful decorations seen in many homes. But they still wanted to celebrate Christ's birth, so on Christmas Eve the children put an evergreen tree in their home, though sadly they had to leave it bare. After everyone had gone to bed, a family of spiders saw what had happened and decided to help.

During the night they spun webs all over the tree, carefully covering it with glistening spider webs looped from branch to branch. When the Christ Child came that night to bless the Christmas trees, he saw the cobwebs and all the work that the kind spiders had done. Then he blessed the poor family's tree, turning the spider webs into beautiful strands of silver and gold garlands. When they awoke to the glorious sight of the tree, they knew that the Christ Child had truly blessed them.

Pine Tree

In the long ago past, the pine tree was like other trees, with green boughs through the spring and summer. When autumn came, its leaves and needles withered, falling to the ground, leaving bare branches throughout the cold winter months. Then one day Mary, Joseph, and the Christ Child, traveling hastily away from Bethlehem to escape King Herod, took shelter from the cold under a pine tree with its many needles. They were very tired from the journey and soon fell asleep.

The small pine tree felt sorry for the little family, sleeping out in the open, on such a cold night. How could he protect them? He realized that if he drooped his branches down around the baby, Mary, and Joseph, he would shelter them from the cold. His branches also hid them from Herod's searching troops throughout the night. In the morning the child awoke safe and warm. He then blessed the little pine tree, saying that it would be ever green, throughout all the year, providing shelter and sanctuary for birds and animals even in the coldest winter days.

Owl

It has long been told that the owl was one of the many birds that the wise men invited to join them as they traveled to greet the newborn Christ Child. All the other birds arose and flew through the dark night to see the child in the manger, while singing in glory and thanks for the little one. But one bird, the owl, warm in his nest, was unwilling to give up his sleep and go into the cold with the others.

Instead he called out sleepily, "Who is this I'm to see? Who? Who?" And then he closed his eyes, refusing to fly

to see the child. He slept through the night and didn't fly with the other birds to find the child in the manger. In the morning the owl was most sorry for what he had missed, as he heard from the other birds what they had seen. And now he cries each evening in remorse, "Who, who will take me to the Christ Child?" He stays awake throughout the dark night, sorry that he hadn't once given up his warm nest to see the baby and be blessed.

Rosemary

When Jesus was born so many years ago, the rosemary bush was a very plain shrub, with neither blossoms nor fragrance. It was just a small green plant. Then one day as Mary, Joseph, and the baby Jesus fled to Egypt to escape King Herod, Mary stopped on their travels to wash some of the Baby's clothes in a stream nearby. There she found a rosemary bush and hung the small garments on it to dry. The plain little plant stood fast all through the day, holding the garments carefully, never bending nor letting them reach the ground and dirt below.

When Mary returned later to gather the clean, dry clothes, she thanked the small plant for its help and strength, and she blessed it. Now the rosemary bush forever bears blue flowers in remembrance of the color that matched Mary's own cloak. And if you find a rosemary plant, you too can smell its sweet fragrance, a gentle reminder of the Christ Child's garments that hung there.

Poinsettia

In a small village in Mexico it was the custom for each person to bring a gift to place on the church's altar on Christmas Eve, in remembrance of the baby Jesus. Many years ago one small orphan child was afraid to go to the church and cried because he didn't have anything special to give. Although he had picked some weeds along the roadside as a gift, he was ashamed to take them inside and place them next to the other fine gifts he saw there.

Suddenly an angel appeared to him and told him to take the dried-up weeds in to the altar for the baby. Still worried,

he did as he had been instructed, and as he placed the boughs there, they suddenly bloomed a dazzling and brilliant scarlet color, the first poinsettia. The small boy's humble offering had been miraculously transformed. The people then called it "The Flower of the Holy Night" or "The Flor de la Noche Buena", its name to this day. Many years later, Ambassador to Mexico Joseph Poinsett found it growing there and brought it to the United States. Today it is a beautiful Christmas decoration in many homes, a reminder of how a lowly gift, from the heart, is the best gift of all.

Star

On that night many years ago when Jesus was born, the heavens were filled with stars. But one star is said to have stood out especially large and bright over the stable where the baby lay. Shepherds who saw it gazed in wonder when the whole sky became light. Traveling with their sheep, they were able to follow the star to the manger. There they saw the Christ Child and realized the star shone because of him.

Far away the three wise men had also seen a star in the East, and it went ahead of them as they traveled to

King Herod. They asked, "Where is the one who has been born the king of the Jews? We saw his star in the East and have come to worship him." Herod was fearful of this prophecy so

he sent the magi to search for the Christ Child. They spent many days following a star to where they finally found him. Now if you go outside an hour or so before dawn at Christmastime and look up in the eastern sky, you too might see a blazing blue-white beacon. Perhaps it is the same light that guided so many to the babe all those years ago.

Wise Men

When Herod, the Roman king of Judea, heard that a child would be born who was to be called King of the Jews, he was greatly threatened. His chief priests and scribes told him that Bethlehem has been prophesied as the place. Herod then secretly summoned three wise men and sent them to search for this baby. He hoped that he could find and destroy the child. As they traveled, Gaspar, Melchior, and Balthasar, who tradition says was a black man from Ethiopia, followed a star in the East.

The star went before them until it came to rest over the place where the Christ Child lay. The three wise men rejoiced with great happiness upon seeing the child, and they fell on their knees and worshiped him. Then, opening their treasures, they offered gold, frankincense, and myrrh, gifts of great value. Soon after, the magi were warned in a dream not to tell Herod about the child, and so they departed for their own countries by another way and did not return to the king.

Camel

When the wise men traveled to find the Christ Child, they brought with them many camels, including one very small young camel, to carry their goods and gifts. It was a long and difficult journey over hot sands and through dry deserts. The littlest camel was very proud to be carrying the gifts to the Christ Child, although he did find it hard to keep up with the larger camels with their long legs. When the wise men with their camels finally arrived at the stable and reached for the gifts to give to the child, they heard a loud thump.

It was the littlest camel, who was so tired that his legs could hold him no longer, and he fell right in front of the babe. Then the baby Jesus reached out his small hand to him, and the camel once again felt strong. Now it is said by children in Syria that the littlest camel makes the same journey each year, bringing gifts to all the children in the name of the greatest king of all, Jesus.

Holy Thorn

Long ago, so the legend says, Joseph of Arimathea, with other early followers of Christ, traveled through western Europe and England. While wandering through the countryside, he told the wondrous story of the Christ Child and his birth in a stable on Christmas Day. One day after preaching, Joseph grew tired and sat down to rest on Wearyall Hill, setting his staff in the ground before he slept.

As he slumbered the limb began to root and grow, and it continued to do so, long after Saint Joseph had continued on his journey. That staff became a hawthorn tree. In England today the Holy Thorn, as it is now known, still blooms at midnight on January 5th, the date of the old-calendar Christmas Eve. It is said to do so in remembrance of Saint Joseph. Today we call it the winter-flowering hawthorn, a beautiful sight on cold days, reminding us of the story of the Christ Child that Joseph brought to many countries.

Santa Claus

Santa Claus is a mostly American legend today, but it is based on many stories of a real fourth-century priest who was kind and generous. He has been known as Saint Nicholas in many countries throughout the world. In Northern Europe many centuries ago, Saint Nicholas was thought to bring gifts down the chimney for deserving children, one of the first of the legends of our Santa today. In England he is known as Father Christmas, and children leave shoes by the door for their small gifts and candy.

Spanish children hope Papa Noel will put gifts in their shoes too, while French children call him Pere Noel, and Bobbo Natale is his name in Italy.

It is thought that Dutch immigrants brought to colonial America the stories of Sinterklaas, which became pronounced as Santa Claus. In 1822 Clement Moore published the beloved poem "The Night Before Christmas," which created the modern image of Santa as a jolly, bearded, fat man dressed in a red suit. The eight reindeer have been joined more recently by Rudolph, and children today still hang their stockings by the chimney for gifts from Santa.

Manger

After they were married, Mary and Joseph lived in Nazareth. The Roman Emperor at that time, Caesar Augustus, wanted a list of all the people in his empire for taxation. He sent out a decree that all the world should be enrolled, each person in his own city. So Joseph and his wife Mary, who was with child, went from the city of Nazareth to Bethlehem where Joseph's family had lived, to be counted.

Mary traveled slowly with Joseph, by donkey and by foot the long distance. When they wearily arrived in Bethlehem, they had to stay in a stable where Mary then gave birth to her son. She wrapped the child in swaddling clothes and laid him in a manger. He had no crib or bed, only a rough wooden trough used to feed cattle and horses. Mary called him Jesus, the name given by the angel before he was conceived in the womb. Wise men and shepherds, animals and birds, all came to the humble manger to worship and give thanks.

Dear Readers,

During every evening of Advent choose a story to read together with your family, then hang the matching ornament. Put the ornaments around the house, on a Christmas tree, or anywhere you'd like to display them. You can read the legends in the order of the book or by children's choices, saving Santa and the Manger for December 24th and 25th. The ornaments can then be kept for years to come in the pocket at the back of the book.

We hope you and your loved ones will enjoy celebrating Advent with these legends.

Judy and Nancy